Quick & Easy Internet Activities
for the One-Computer Classroom

Space

by Mary Kay Carson

20 Fun, Web-Based Activities
With Reproducible Graphic Organizers That Enable Kids to Learn
the Very Latest Information—On Their Own!

SCHOLASTIC
PROFESSIONAL BOOKS

New York • Toronto • London • Auckland • Sydney • Mexico City • New Dehli • Hong Kong

Cover design by **George Myer**

Interior design by **Holly Grundon**

Interior illustrations by **Ivy Rutzky**

Cover image: Web page used with permission of the Jet Propulsion Laboratory/NASA-California Institute of Technology

ISBN: 0-439-24441-2

Contents

Using This Book

Welcome to *Quick & Easy Internet Activities for the One-Computer Classroom: Space!* The 20 activities in this book will expand your students' knowledge of stars, moons, planets, comets, and space exploration, and build their Internet skills at the same time. The World Wide Web is the perfect resource for teaching a unit on space. On the Web, students can read about the latest discoveries, such as new planets, and see the most amazing images, such as an exploding star. Students can literally witness history in the making!

What's Inside

This book is divided into four chapters: Stars and Our Sun; Planets and Moons; Comets, Meteoroids, and Asteroids; and Space Exploration. Each of the 20 activities in this book comes with a teacher page, filled with background information, step-by-step mini-lessons, and extension activities. Reproducible student pages provide simple directions, graphic organizers, and recording sheets that help students complete Web-based activities, from simple scavenger hunts to projects that involve higher-level critical thinking.

Accessing the Web Sites

As you may already know, gaining access to Web sites can be potentially frustrating. Sites come and go faster than it takes to publish a book. In addition, some of the URLs (Uniform Resource Locators, or the site's address) are so long and unwieldy, it's easy to type in the wrong letter or symbol. When it comes to the Web, one wrong letter can give you an error message or, worse, land you (or your students) in an undesirable site.

To access the Web sites for the activities in this book, go to:
www.scholastic.com/profbooks /netexplorations/space.htm

Simply click on the activity name to go directly to the appropriate Web site needed to complete the activity. No more typing, no more worrying about whether or not the site is still up.

You may still want to check out the Web sites yourself before using them in the day's activity. This way, you'll be familiar with the sites and know where to steer students to find the information they need.

Fitting the Internet Into Your Classroom

D o you have only one wired computer in your classroom? Or are you one of the lucky few who have computer labs where all students can go online at the same time? Either way, you'll have no problems adapting the activities in this book to your specific computer setup! The activities are designed so that students won't need to spend too much time on the Internet—a PLUS for the one-computer classroom!

Every activity has an at-the-computer component that requires Web access. The rest of the activity can usually be completed away from the computer. Most activities can also be done by students in small groups—another time-saving feature. To ensure that students use their limited time on the Web effectively, make certain they have a clear, focused objective of what they are looking for before they go to the computer. When they go online, students should find and jot down the information they need, then leave the computer to let others have a turn. (If you do have access to extra computers and would like to extend your students' computer skills, you may want to encourage them to use graphics and publishing software, such as Kid Pix or HyperStudio, to enhance their projects.)

Here are more tips for managing the one-computer classroom:

Taking Turns

Assign individual students or small student groups about 15 minutes of computer time in rotation. (The amount of time depends on how long you think it will take them to get their task done.) Have the rest of the class complete the non-computer part of the activity, or give them related activities to do while waiting for their turn at the computer.

Hooking Up a Projector

You can hook up your computer to a video monitor or a projector, and have your whole class browse the Web together. Students can participate by taking turns clicking on hyperlinks or reading the information.

Using Offline Software

Offline tool software, such as Web Whacker (**www.bluesquirrel.com**), can capture all the pages in a Web site and download it. Students can then view the Web site from computers that aren't hooked to the Internet. You can also save Web pages as viewable documents and/or print them out, but they will likely be void of pictures and graphics.

More Tips for Smooth Surfing

★ Review with students the basics of using their Internet browsers, such as typing in exact URLs, scrolling, going back and forward between Web pages, using hyperlinks, printing, and copying and pasting images.

★ Consider creating "Browser Basics" help sheets or index cards and post them near the computer.

★ Many Web sites can contain an overwhelming barrage of information. Encourage students to "browse" the Web sites for the information they need, and not worry about reading everything.

Making the Internet Safe for Children

The profusion of chat room weirdoes, anonymous e-mails, and pornography makes many parents and teachers wary about their kids using the Internet—with good reason. This section provides some help. (Note: You might combine some or all of the following points into an "Appropriate Use Policy" for posting in the classroom and for students to read, sign, and take home.) Here are two ways to avoid inappropriate materials.

Close Supervision
Closely supervise students while they work on the computer. Remind students that working on a computer is a privilege, one that can be taken away if abused.

Blocking or Filtering Software
If you'd like to install software that blocks students' access to inappropriate Web sites, here are some common sources:

> teams.lacoe.edu/documentation /Internet/security/software.html

> coverage.cnet.com/Content/Reviews /Compare/Safesurf/

> www.netparents.org/parentstips /browsers.html

Rules for Staying Safe on the Net

Do Tell
Students should immediately report to you if they receive a message that seems inappropriate or makes them feel uncomfortable. They should NEVER respond to such messages. They should also report to you if they come across an inappropriate Web site.

Don't Tell
Students should NEVER give out personal information in chat rooms and e-mails, such as their phone numbers, last names, addresses, or personal descriptions, without permission from you or their parents.

Don't Show
Students should NEVER send photographs to e-acquaintances without permission from you or their parents.

Don't Go
Students should NEVER agree to get together with someone they meet online without permission from you or their parents. Even with parental permission and accompaniment, caution should be taken.

Chaperoned Only
Students should go only to chat rooms that are age-appropriate and supervised.

Evaluating Internet Sources

The Internet is a great research tool for both you and your students. While the Web sites you'll use for this book have been selected for their accuracy and age-appropriateness, you'll no doubt come across other Web sites during your Internet explorations. But how will you—or your students—know whether or not the information found there is accurate? Here are some tips for evaluating Internet sources:

Where is it coming from? Is the page sponsored by a trustworthy source, such as a government office, university, or non-profit organization? If it's unclear who sponsors the Web site, try to find an "About This Site" hyperlink to find out.

Who wrote it? Is an author given for the site? Are his or her qualifications stated? Is there information on how to contact the author?

How accurate is the information? Are sources for the information provided or cited? Does it seem outdated or not very exact? Is there a publishing and/or a last-updated date? Are charts and graphs labeled? Is the Web page complete or still "under construction"? Does it look "professional"— free of spelling errors and typos?

What's the angle? Does the information seem like it's trying to persuade you, or is it presented in an even manner? Are there advertisements on the Web site? Whether the information is provided as an educational or public service, or as a venue for promoting a product can make a difference in its content and objectivity. Sticking to Web sites with URLs that end in **.gov, .edu,** or **.org** is often safer, though not foolproof. Many non-profit organizations have an agenda to push, and some for-profit companies provide reliable and accurate information on the Internet.

Be choosy! If the Web site and/or information seems suspect, it very likely is! If you can't corroborate a fact found on the Web site with any other source, it's probably not true.

Meeting the Science Standards

The information and lessons featured in this book meet many of the National Science Education Content Standards:

Grades K–4
★ Position and motion of objects
★ Properties of earth materials
★ Objects in the sky
★ Changes in earth and sky
★ Abilities of technological design
★ Understandings about science and technology
★ Science as a human endeavor

Grades 5–8
★ Motions and forces
★ Structure of the earth system
★ Earth's history
★ Earth in the solar system
★ Abilities of technological design
★ Understandings about science and technology
★ Natural hazards
★ Science as a human endeavor
★ History of science

Science

Here Comes the Sun!

Students gather facts about our sun and complete a diagram and chart.

BACKGROUND

Our sun is a middle-aged, average-sized, medium-hot, yellow star. It is the closest star to Earth and the largest celestial body in our solar system. Like all stars, the sun is a ball of spinning hot gases. It is made of mostly hydrogen and helium, and produces energy by a *nuclear fusion reaction* in its center, or *core*. The *corona* is the outer part of the sun's atmosphere.

DOING THE ACTIVITY

1. Engage students in a discussion about the sun. Find out what they know about our closest star. Ask students: Why is the sun hot? Why is it important to life?

2. Photocopy and distribute page 9 to each student or student pair who will be working at a computer.

3. Have students visit the Web sites and conduct research to complete the sun diagram and chart. Encourage students to find extra hot facts about the sun to add to their charts as well.

ANSWERS *(Answers may vary slightly depending on the Web site.)*

1. corona   **2.** surface   **3.** core   **4.** 4.5 billion years

5. 93,026,724 miles or 149,680,000 km   **6.** 1,392,000 km

7. 9,900°F, 5,500°C, or 5770°K   **8.** hydrogen and helium

9. yellow   **10.** nuclear fusion

More To Do:

Sun Prints

Students can witness the strength of sunlight by creating sun prints. Have students arrange small objects of different shapes (coins, leaves, books, etc.) onto colored construction paper. Apply weight to the objects, if necessary. Set the paper on a sunny windowsill and leave it there for a week. Then invite students to remove the objects and see the shapes left behind. The paper's dyes break down when exposed to sunlight.

Name(s) _____ Date _____

Meet the Sun!

How much do you know about the star of our solar system? Conduct research on the Web to help you label the sun diagram here and write a hot fact about each layer of the sun. Then fill out the chart and add another fact related to each question.

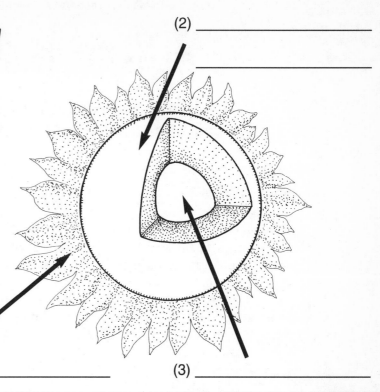

(2) _____
_____

(1) _____

(3) _____
_____

	SUN FACTS	SUPER-HOT FACT
(4) How old is the sun?		The sun is expected to last another 4–5 billion years.
(5) How far is it from the Earth?		
(6) What is its diameter?		
(7) What is its surface temperature?		
(8) What is it made of?		
(9) What color is it?		
(10) How does it produce energy?		

Science
Language
Arts
Art

A Star Is Born

Students learn about the life stages of stars and create a star life-cycle mobile.

BACKGROUND:

Stars are born in *stellar nurseries* made of clouds of dust and gas called *nebulae*. Gases clump into young stars inside these clouds and mature as they spin faster and heat up. The rest of a star's life cycle depends on its size. Stars the same size as our sun swell to *red giants* before cooling to *planetary nebula*, then *white dwarf stars*, and finally *black dwarfs*. Huge stars explode into *supernova* and shed most of their mass to become *neutron stars*. An even bigger star collapses into a *black hole*, where gravity is so strong, even light can't escape.

DOING THE ACTIVITY

1. Introduce the idea that stars have life cycles to students. Ask: Where do stars come from? Do they last forever? What happens when they burn out? Remind students that stars come in different sizes. Explain that the life stages a star goes through depend on its size.

2. Photocopy and distribute page 11 to each student, student pair, or small group completing the activity. Tell students that they'll be making a mobile of a star's life cycle.

3. Invite students to choose the size star they want to work on—a sun-size star or a giant star. Have students research their star's life cycle on the Web, then cut out the life stages for their star and put them in order. On the back of each stage, have them write what happens during that stage and how long it lasts.

4. Provide hangers, scissors, yarn or string, and tape so students can create a mobile of their star's life cycle. Invite students to color their star shapes and create a title label for the mobiles.

More To Do:

My Life as a Star

Invite students to write the life story of a star in the first person.
Encourage them to mix fantasy with facts.

A Starry Mobile

Choose the size star you want to study—
a sun-size star or a giant star. Learn about
the life of your size star on the Web. Then
cut out the life stages you need below and
put them in order. Write on the back of each
box what happens during that stage of your
star's life. Finally, design a mobile showing
your star's life cycle.

STELLAR NURSERY

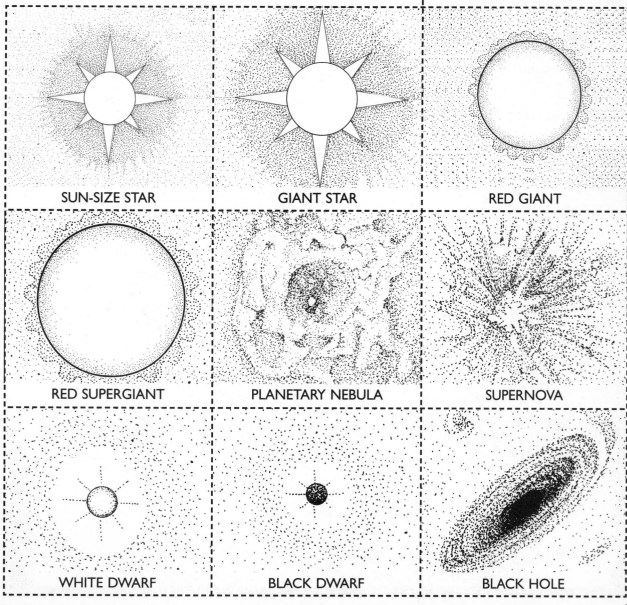

SUN-SIZE STAR

GIANT STAR

RED GIANT

RED SUPERGIANT

PLANETARY NEBULA

SUPERNOVA

WHITE DWARF

BLACK DWARF

BLACK HOLE

Science
Social
Studies
Language
Arts

Starry Stories

Students investigate a number of constellation mythologies and write one of their own.

BACKGROUND

A *constellation* is a group of bright stars that forms a recognizable pattern when viewed from Earth. The stars that make up a constellation are not necessarily close to each other out in space. Constellations are cultural, not scientific, phenomena. Throughout history and across cultures, people have looked at the night sky, seen these patterns in the stars, and created stories to explain the hunters, animals, gods, and beings imagined there.

DOING THE ACTIVITY

1. Draw the Big Dipper on the board and use it as a discussion starter about constellations and their mythologies to prepare students for the activity.

2. Photocopy and distribute page 13 to each student.

3. Have students browse on the Web and read a number of mythologies about the origins of constellations. Have them begin thinking about a constellation they would like to write about.

4. Invite students to fill out the graphic organizer to plan their stories. Have them fill out the name of the constellation they've chosen, the characters, setting, problem, and solution. If possible, have students print out an image of their chosen constellation to accompany their stories.

5. When children have finished writing their myths, consider grouping the stories by constellation and displaying them on a wall or bulletin board for students to compare.

More To Do:

Salty Constellations

Invite students to create their chosen constellations on black construction paper. They can glue chunks of rock salt to represent the stars.

A Story of Stars

Visit the Web to find out what starry myths people around the world tell. Then choose a constellation and write a myth of your own. Fill out this graphic organizer to help you plan your story. Then, write your story on the back of this page.

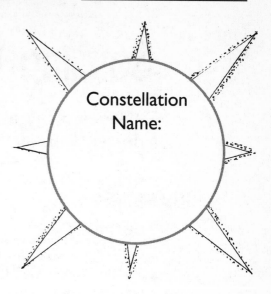

Constellation Name:

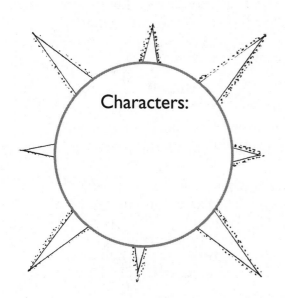

Characters:

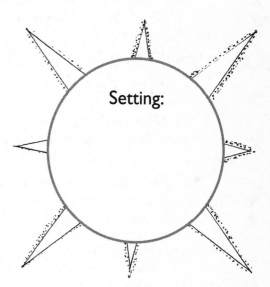

Setting:

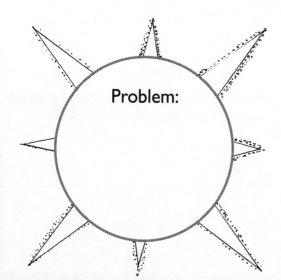

Problem:

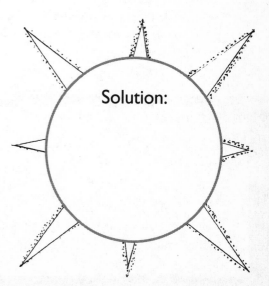

Solution:

Science
Math

Sorting Out Galaxies

Students learn about the different kinds of galaxies and sort them according to shape.

BACKGROUND

A *galaxy* is a large assembly of stars, gas, and dust, all held together by gravity. Galaxies come in three main shapes: *spiral, elliptical,* and *irregular.* A spiral galaxy is shaped like a disk with a bulge in the center and spiral arms that coil out. Our own galaxy, the Milky Way, is a spiral galaxy. Elliptical galaxies range in shape from almost-perfect spheres to flattened globes. Irregular galaxies have no particular shape at all.

DOING THE ACTIVITY

1. Ask students if they've ever seen our galaxy, the Milky Way. Use the discussion to define a galaxy and introduce the idea that galaxies come in different shapes.

2. Photocopy and distribute page 15 to each student, student pair, or small group doing the activity.

3. Have students visit the Web sites to collect and sort different types of galaxies. (Students can draw pictures of the galaxies in their charts instead of printing them out.) When labeling their galaxies, remind students that many galaxies have letter/number designations, such as M100 or NGC 3034, instead of or in addition to regular names. Encourage them to write down both kinds of names, if available.

4. Invite the class to pool their findings of galaxies into a gallery. Challenge students to give descriptive names to the galaxies that have only letter/number designations.

More To Do:

Galactic Art

Galaxies are three-dimensional objects. Challenge students to create galaxy shapes in 3-D using clay, Styrofoam, or other art materials.

Name(s) _____ Date _____

Galaxy Hunt

Go on a galaxy quest to discover different galaxy shapes—spiral, elliptical, and irregular. Collect and print several images of each shape from the Web. Then sort the images and glue them to the appropriate circles below. Don't forget to label the galaxies with their names.

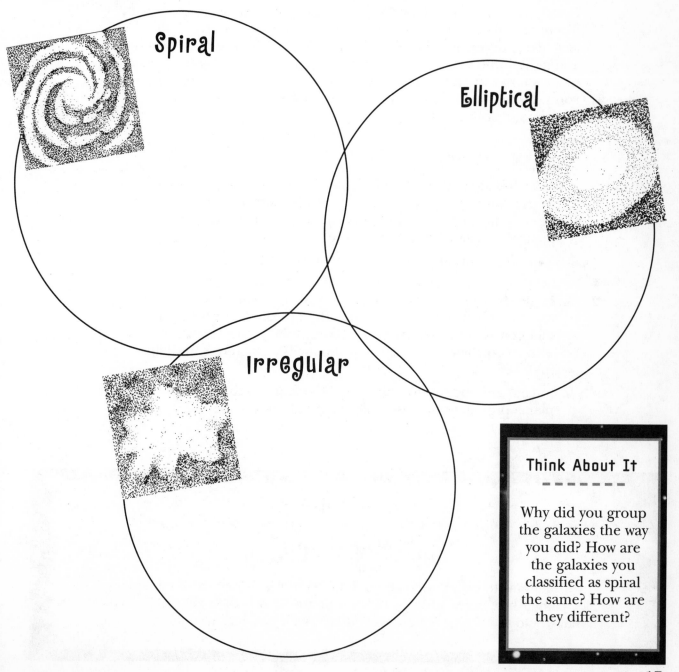

Spiral

Elliptical

Irregular

Think About It

- - - - - - -

Why did you group the galaxies the way you did? How are the galaxies you classified as spiral the same? How are they different?

Science
Language
Arts

Solar System Tourism

Students gather information about one of the planets and create a travel brochure inviting visitors to that world.

BACKGROUND

Planets are large celestial bodies that orbit around a star, like our sun. There are nine planets in our solar system. Mercury, Venus, Earth, and Mars are small rocky planets that orbit close to the sun's heat and light. Jupiter, Saturn, Uranus, and Neptune are *gas giants*—huge planets made up of thick atmospheres, dense liquid, and small rocky cores. Pluto is a unique, cold, and dark world, probably with a solid surface of frozen gases.

DOING THE ACTIVITY

1. Ask students: If you were to visit any other planet in our solar system, which would it be? Engage students in a discussion about when humans will visit another planet. Ask: What will visiting the planet be like? What will visitors see?

2. Photocopy and distribute page 17 to each student, student pair, or small group.

3. Invite students to choose a planet to write about. Have students research their planet on the Web, then create a travel brochure that points out the different features of the planet. Provide them with scissors and crayons, colored pencils, or markers to design their brochure.

4. Encourage students to share their brochures with the class or plan a presentation that would entice tourists to visit their planet of choice.

More To Do:

Planetary Itinerary

Invite students to plan and write up detailed tourist itineraries to the planets their brochures advertise. How long would it take to get there? What would the accommodations be like? What activities would be offered?

Off-World Vacation Destination

Why visit Venus or stop off at Saturn? Use the Web to help create a fact-filled vacation brochure to another planet. Fill in the blanks below with information you've learned about the planet. Then design your brochure by cutting it out and folding it in half along the dotted line. Write a title and draw a picture on the front of your brochure that "sells" your planet to tourists.

Come visit _____ !

Want to know more about _____

_____ ?

Here are some out-of-this-world facts!

★ The days are _____ long.

★ A year lasts _____ .

★ There are _____ moons.

★ It does/doesn't have rings.

★ Its distance across, or diameter, is

_____ .

★ _____

★ _____

★ _____

★ _____

The weather is pretty unusual! It's

_____

_____

_____

There's lots to do and amazing sites to

see, including:

★ _____

★ _____

★ _____

★ _____

But the most important reason you

should visit _____ is that

_____

_____ !

Science

Name That Moon!

Students create flash cards with questions and answers about one of the solar system's many moons.

BACKGROUND

A *moon*, or natural satellite, is an object that orbits a planet or large asteroid. All the planets of our solar system have moons, except Mercury and Venus. Moons vary greatly in size and composition. Some are dead worlds pockmarked with ancient craters, while others are covered with active volcanoes and have thin atmospheres.

DOING THE ACTIVITY

1. Photocopy and distribute page 19 to each student, student pair, or small group, and assign each a moon. Check out the Web sites to get a list of all the named moons of the solar system.

2. Hold a discussion with students about moons. Ask: What is a moon? Are all moons like Earth's moon? Why or why not?

3. Have students conduct research on the Web to create flash cards filled with information about their chosen moon. Provide them with scissors to cut apart the cards.

4. Invite students to quiz each other about the solar system's moons using the flash cards they've just completed.

More To Do:

Moon Life

Many of the large moons of the gas-giant planets are geologically active. These volcano-, ocean-, and ice-covered worlds may be the most-likely candidates for harboring life in our solar system. Invite student groups to choose one of the moons, speculate on what kind of life could exist there, and plan a mission to find out. Moon candidates for this project include: Jupiter's Io, Europa, and Ganymede, as well as Saturn's Dione, Titan, Tethys, and Enceladus.

Name(s) ______________________ Date ______________

Flashy Moons

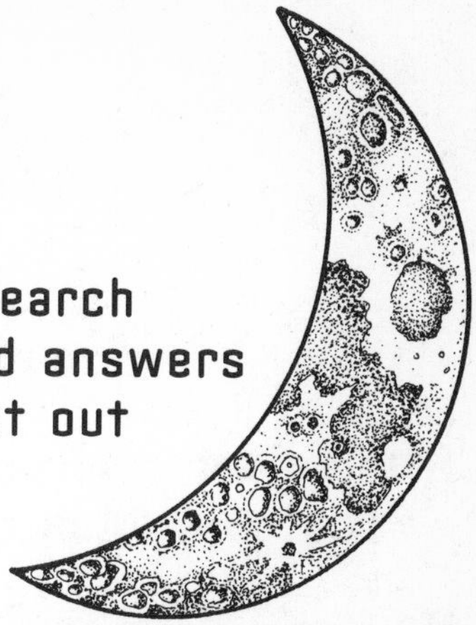

Pick one of the moons in our solar system and research cool facts about it on the Web. Write questions and answers about your moon on the flash cards below. Then cut out the cards and use them to quiz your classmates.

Moon Question:

What planet does the moon

______________________ orbit?

Answer:

____

____

____

Moon Question:

____

____

Answer:

____

____

____

Moon Question:

____

____

Answer:

____

____

____

Moon Question:

____

____

Answer:

____

____

____

Science
Math

Scaling Down the Solar System

Students research and record the distances of the nine planets from the sun, then create a scaled-down model of the solar system.

BACKGROUND

Models of the solar system abound, but most are not to scale. A true-to-scale model of the solar system's distances and planet sizes wouldn't even fit inside a room. If the sun were the size of a baseball sitting on home plate, Pluto would be a grain of sand just outside the ballpark!

DOING THE ACTIVITY

1. You may want to review the metric system with students, if needed. They'll be using kilometers, meters, centimeters, and millimeters to measure out a scale model of the solar system.

2. Photocopy and distribute page 21 to each student pair or small group. Have students find the distances for column 1 on the Web. Then have them complete the chart, giving assistance when needed. Provide students with calculators.

3. Once the charts are finished, decide the size of the models to be made. Look at the Pluto's distance (the farthest planet) in columns 4, 5, and 6 to determine the size of your scale model. Using data from column 4, for example, you'll need about 6 meters of floor or wall space.

4. Provide students with materials to create a scale model of the distances. Remember that the sizes of the planets themselves will NOT be to scale. Have students mark where the sun would be as a starting point, then measure from the sun to each planet. Then have them add a construction-paper sun and planets. Have students stagger the position of the planets along their orbits.

More To Do:

More Math

Challenge students to graph each planet's distance vs. its year (the time it takes to complete an orbit around the sun in Earth years). Is there a relationship? What is it?

We Shrank the Solar System!

The solar system is a big place! Here's how you can make it fit on a poster or a wall. Conduct research on the Web to fill in column 1 of the chart below. (HINT: Use the average or mean distance, not the shortest or longest distance.) Then use a calculator to fill in the rest of the chart. Your teacher will help you choose which scale to use to build a model of the solar system, using column 4, 5, or 6.

Planet	(1) Distance from sun in kilometers (km)	(2) Divide (1) by ten million	(3) Round (2) to whole number	(4) Write (3) as cm (1 unit equals 1 cm)	(5) Divide (4) by two (1 unit equals 0.5 cm)	(6) Write (3) as mm (1 unit equals 1 mm)
Mercury	57,900,000	5.79	6	6 cm	3 cm	6 mm
Venus						
Earth						
Mars						
Jupiter						
Saturn						
Uranus						
Neptune						
Pluto	5,900,100,000	590.01	590	590 cm (~6 m)	295 cm (~3 m)	590 mm (59 cm)

Science
Critical
Thinking

Creature From Another Planet

Students use facts they gather about a planet to create an alien adapted to living there.

BACKGROUND

Finding intelligent life in our own small solar system seems unlikely, but discovering the remains of simple life forms on Mars or a gas giant's large moon seems very possible. Scientists are uncovering life in extreme earth environments, lending evidence to life's adaptability and resilience.

DOING THE ACTIVITY

1. Engage students in a discussion about extraterrestrial life. Point out that life forms have been found in many inhospitable environments on Earth. Giant tubeworms thrive around deep-sea vents where sunlight never reaches, and bacteria live in boiling hot springs. Emphasize that life must be adapted to its environment to survive.

2. Photocopy and distribute page 23 to each student. Assign a planet to students or let them choose one. Invite students to complete the chart and think about how a life form would have to be adapted to live on their planet.

3. Provide students with paper and art materials to draw or paint their aliens. You may also want to encourage students to draw their aliens on the computer using Kid Pix or any other graphics software. Have students present their aliens to the class and explain why they chose to outfit their aliens with the adaptations they did.

More To Do:

Share an Alien

Invite students to e-mail written descriptions of their created aliens to e-pals, challenge the recipients to draw the aliens based on the descriptions, and then send the actual drawings for comparison. You can set up e-pals for students through other teachers, or through **www.epals.com** on the Web.

Name(s) _____   Date _____

Alien Creation

If life were found on another planet, what
would it look like? Investigate the conditions
on a planet in our solar system on the Web.
Fill out the chart below. Then draw an alien
that would be adapted to live there on the
back of this page.

Planet: _____

Planetary Conditions	Alien Adaptation Needed to Survive These Conditions
How much gravity is there compared to Earth? _____	
How far is it from the sun? _____	
What is the atmosphere made of? _____	
What is the average temperature? _____	
What is the weather like? (Is it windy, stormy, etc.?) _____	
What is the surface like? (Does it have oceans, volcanoes, mountains, etc?) _____	

Science
Social
Studies

From Apollo to Luna Base

Students gather facts about the moon and plan the first moon colony.

BACKGROUND

In 1969, Neil Armstrong became the first human to walk on the moon. The Apollo missions ended in 1972, and no human has set foot on the moon since. Many believe the next time we return it will be to stay. Supporters say a permanent base on the moon is the next logical step to traveling the solar system and beyond. The base would provide needed long-term research into living in a space environment and serve as an off-world launch site.

DOING THE ACTIVITY

1. Poll students to find out who would like to live on the moon. Ask students: What would you need to live on the moon?

2. Photocopy and distribute page 25 to each student pair or small group. Have them research some basic facts about the moon before they plan their moon colony.

3. Have students fill out their Moon Colony Plans and draw their maps. If time allows, have students draw a more detailed schematic of one of the buildings or modules.

4. Have the groups share their plans and drawings with the class. Ask students to observe the similarities and differences.

ANSWERS *(Moon Facts)*

1. 15 percent or 1/6th of Earth's gravity   **2.** Ice exists at poles.

3. no   **4.** no   **5.** The surface is dusty, rocky, and filled with craters.

6. day temperatures: 107°C to 214°C; night temperatures: −184°C to −153°C

More To Do:

Lunar Diary

Invite students to keep a diary for one week,
recording the day-to-day life on a moon colony.

Name(s) _____ Date _____

Moon Town

If humans moved to the moon, what would we need to pack and how would we live? Conduct research on the Web to find answers to the Moon Facts questions. Think about how these conditions would affect setting up a colony on the moon. Then create a Moon Colony Plan and draw a map of your colony on the back of this paper.

Moon Facts

1. How much gravity does the moon have compared to Earth? _____

2. Is there water or ice? _____

3. Is there an atmosphere? _____

4. Is there breathable air? _____

5. What is the surface like? _____

6. What is the temperature during the day _____ and night _____?

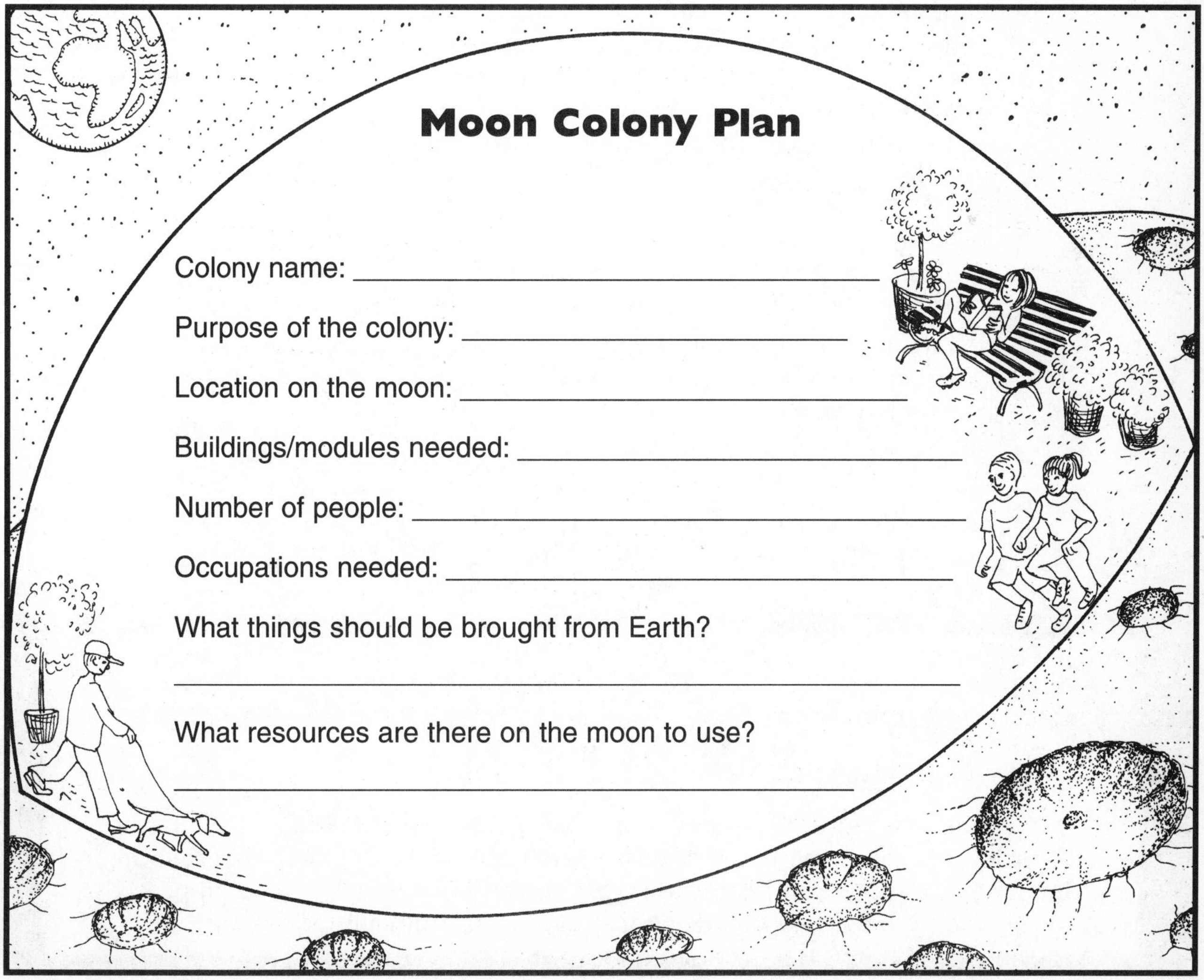

Moon Colony Plan

Colony name: _____

Purpose of the colony: _____

Location on the moon: _____

Buildings/modules needed: _____

Number of people: _____

Occupations needed: _____

What things should be brought from Earth?

_____

What resources are there on the moon to use?

_____

Science
Language
Arts
Social
Studies

Halley's Comet: Past and Future

Students use Web sites to gather information about comets and then write a letter about seeing Halley's Comet in 2062.

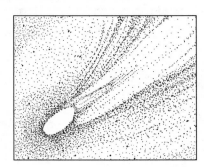

BACKGROUND

Comets are icy space objects that orbit the sun. A comet has a solid nucleus or center made up of ice and rocky dust particles. When a comet nears the sun, some of the ice vaporizes, causing gases and particles stuck in the ice to fly away from the sun and form the atmosphere, or *coma*, and tail of the comet. We see comets because their flying dust reflects sunlight.

DOING THE ACTIVITY

1. Ask students if anyone has ever seen a comet? (A few may remember Comet Hale-Bopp of 1997.) What does it look like? Use the discussion to assess students' knowledge of comets.

2. Photocopy and distribute page 27 to each student. Have students conduct research on the Web to find answers to the questions on the student page.

3. If the whole class is doing the activity, consider having a class discussion about life in 2062. Encourage students to use their imaginations! Then invite students to write their letters, incorporating their ideas and the information they found about comets.

More To Do:

Halley's History

Challenge students to create a time line that highlights each of Halley's recorded returns, using the Web for research. Encourage students to label the time line with important historical events around the time the comet appeared and note the people's reactions to the comet at each of its visits.

Letter from the Future

The year is 2062 and you just saw Halley's Comet! Write a letter to your grandchild telling him or her about comets in general, Halley's Comet, and what it was like seeing this famous comet. Use the Web to find the answers to the questions at right and include the information in your letter:

★ What is a comet?
★ Where does it come from?
★ What does a comet look like?
★ Why do some comets return?
★ Why is Halley's Comet so famous?
★ How often does Halley's Comet return?
★ How is life in 2062 different from life in 1986, the last time Halley's Comet was seen from Earth?

Summer 2062

Dear _____,

Last night I saw Halley's Comet! _____

_____

_____

_____

_____

_____

_____

Love,

Your grand _____ _____

Science

Asteroid Word Search

Students use the Web to find answers to the word-search puzzle questions.

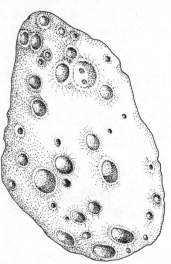

BACKGROUND

Asteroids are rocky fragments leftover from the formation of our solar system. These so-called minor planets or planetoids orbit the sun, mostly within a belt between Mars and Jupiter. The asteroid belt contains an estimated 50,000 asteroids, with more than 1,150 of them larger than 18 miles (30 kilometers) in diameter. Some asteroids are large enough to even have moons!

DOING THE ACTIVITY

1. Photocopy and distribute page 29 to each student or student pair.

2. Have students use the Web to complete the word-search activity.

ANSWERS

1. asteroids   **6.** Greek

2. belt   **7.** orbit

3. Ceres   **8.** Dactyl

4. Mars   **9.** Rendezvous

5. rock   **10.** craters

More To Do:

Asteroid Origins

Challenge students to investigate where asteroids in the asteroid belt originated. Have them present one of the theories and the evidence to support it.

Asteroid Search

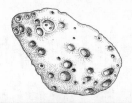

Do asteroids wear belts, have moons, or speak Greek? Conduct research on the Web to find the answers in this fun word search. (The words can be up, down, sideways, or diagonal.)

R	A	M	P	Y	O	E	G	Z	G
C	E	R	E	S	R	Q	R	W	A
J	S	N	T	L	B	R	E	F	S
C	I	R	D	E	I	B	E	L	T
R	T	Y	A	E	T	U	K	I	E
A	R	O	C	K	Z	O	N	P	R
T	U	A	T	S	D	V	F	W	O
E	C	O	Y	J	B	H	O	G	I
R	B	K	L	M	A	R	S	U	D
S	X	C	D	L	H	V	K	Q	S

Questions:

1. These chunks of rock are leftovers of the solar system's formation.

2. Most asteroids are found in an area in space called the asteroid _____.

3. What's the name of the largest asteroid yet found?

4. Most of our solar system's asteroids are between two planets, Jupiter and _____.

5. What's the main ingredient in an asteroid?

6. The word asteroid means "starlike" in what language?

7. Asteroids usually revolve, or _____, around the sun.

8. What is the name of asteroid Ida's moon?

9. NASA's spacecraft to study asteroids was called NEAR, or Near-Earth Asteroid _____.

10. Like Earth's moon, many asteroids are pockmarked with what?

Science Language Arts

Meteor, Meteorite, or Meteoroid?

Students discover the difference between a meteor, meteorite, and meteoroid.

BACKGROUND

Meteoroids are small chunks of rock that travel in space. Many are pieces of crushed asteroids or fragments of comet centers. When a meteoroid enters the Earth's atmosphere, it burns up from the air's friction. The resulting streak of light is called a "shooting star," or *meteor*. A meteor is most visible in the dark of night, especially after midnight. If the meteor doesn't burn up completely, it falls to Earth and becomes a *meteorite*. Tons of meteorites—most smaller than tiny grains of sand—fall to Earth every day.

DOING THE ACTIVITY

1. Prepare students for the activity by asking them if they've ever seen a shooting star. Ask: Is it really a star? Explain that a shooting star is really a chunk of space rock that's traveling through the layer of air that surrounds the Earth.

2. Photocopy and distribute page 31 to each student pair or group. Have them use the Web sites to learn more about the difference between a meteor, meteorite, and a meteoroid.

3. Challenge students to use what they've learned to correct the reporter's article about a space rock that crash-landed on Earth.

More To Do:

Martian Meteorites

Scientists have recently discovered chunks of Martian rock in Antarctica. These rocks arrived on Earth as meteorites. Invite student groups to investigate how the Martian rocks got here and what scientists are learning about the Red Planet from them.

Meteor News

Below is a reporter's account of an out-of-this-world rock that crash-landed on Earth. Check out the Web to learn more about meteors, meteoroids, and meteorites. Then, correct the "facts" and rewrite the reporter's story.

Space Rock Plumments to Earth
Amazingly, no one was hurt!

Yesterday afternoon, a meteor slammed right in the middle of Mr. Pendleton's yard in Starstruck, Alabama. Luckily, no one was hurt. Witnesses say they saw a bright streak of light, or "shooting star," plummet toward the Earth just seconds before the ice-cold rock crashed. Local experts claim this "shooting star" or meteorite may have come from a nearby star.

Scientists say that tons of meteoroids fall toward Earth every day. Most of them burn up in the atmosphere and never reach the Earth's surface. Like most meteoroids that do reach the ground, the one that landed in Mr. Pendleton's yard is as big as a basketball. Mr. Pendleton plans to donate the sizeable rock to the science museum.

Science Critical Thinking

Prepare for Impact!

Students learn about impact events and their causes. Then they brainstorm ideas to prevent disaster, charting the pros and cons of two different plans.

BACKGROUND

Comets and asteroids cross paths with the planets and at times crash into their surfaces. Our moon's pockmarked surface bears evidence to these impacts as do craters on Earth. While many impacts are hardly noticeable, large impacts do happen. Scientists believe that 65 million years ago a comet or asteroid crashed into the Yucatan peninsula, killing off dinosaurs. Astronomers now regularly scan the skies for comets and asteroids whose paths may cross too close to our own.

DOING THE ACTIVITY

1. Start a discussion about comets or asteroids hitting the Earth. Emphasize that while tiny meteorites hit the Earth every day, a giant impact event happens every million years or so.

2. Photocopy and distribute page 33 to each small group.

3. Have students visit the Web to learn about impact events and brainstorm two plans to protect the Earth from a catastrophic impact. Encourage students to take notes on what they find. Once they've chosen a best plan, provide them with art materials to draw a diagram of their plan.

4. Have each group present its strongest plan to the class. Once all the groups have presented, consider taking a vote to choose the best Impact Prevention Strategy Plan.

More To Do:

Homemade Craters

Fill a shallow pan with 6 cups each of flour and salt, and mix them together. Smooth out the top with an index card, then shake cinnamon on top. Have students drop different-size marbles from a height of 12 inches onto the flour mix one at a time, and measure the width of each resulting crater. Have them record their data and compare the numbers.

Name(s) _____ Date _____

Save Earth!

Make a plan to save the Earth from the impact of a giant asteroid!
Search the Web to learn about impact events, and think about two
different ways to protect the Earth from future impacts. Fill out
the diagram below. With your group, choose the plan that would
work best. Then draw a diagram on the back of this page explaining
in more detail how your best plan would work.

Plan A: _____

How does it work?

_____

_____

Why it will work:

_____

_____

Why it may not work:

_____

_____

_____

Plan B: _____

How does it work?

_____

_____

Why it will work:

_____

_____

Why it may not work:

_____

_____

_____

Space Probes to the Planets

Students choose a space probe, find out about its mission, then write a mission report.

BACKGROUND

No one has ever been to another planet. Yet we know a lot about Martian mountains, Venetian volcanoes, and storms on Saturn—thanks to space probes. These robotic spacecraft have visited all the planets of the solar system (except Pluto) as well as asteroids, moons, and comets. These marvels of space travel have plunged into atmospheres, orbited moons, and landed on the frozen plains of faraway worlds, sending back pictures and information.

DOING THE ACTIVITY

1. Start the activity by engaging students in a discussion of what they know about the solar system. Ask: How did we learn so much about the planets, moons, and asteroids in our solar system? Introduce the idea of space probes, emphasizing that they are robotic (unpiloted) craft.

2. Photocopy and distribute page 35 to each student or student pair. Have students choose a probe to report on, or assign them one. You may want to list acceptable choices on the board, eliminating non-probe missions, such as Apollo. If a space probe was scheduled for several missions (e.g. Galileo-Jupiter; Galileo-Asteroid; Galileo-Io; etc.), specify a mission destination for the probe. Students should report on only one mission destination.

3. Have students fill out their Mission Reports using the Web sites.

4. If multiple students have reported on the same space probe mission, invite them to compare their findings.

More To Do:

All About Earth

The two Voyager probes have now left the solar system. They both carry pictures and music about Earth for any aliens that may encounter them one day. Invite student groups to create their own diskettes of information about Earth using multimedia software such as HyperStudio.

Name(s) _____ Date _____

Probes to the Planets

Use Web sites to find out about the journey of a space probe. Then complete the mission report below.

Mission Report

_____
(name of probe)

Launch date: _____

Where did it go? _____

When did it arrive? _____

How long did it take to get there? _____

How far was it from Earth? _____

Did the probe fly by, land on, or orbit the planet/moon/asteroid?

_____

What did it study? _____

How? _____

What new discoveries did it make? _____

What are some interesting facts about the mission?

_____

_____

Science
Language
Arts
Art

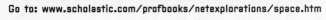

Window on the Universe

Students discover the amazing photographs the Hubble Space Telescope has taken and use one to create a descriptive postcard.

BACKGROUND

Humans have had a blurry view of space since the first telescopes were invented nearly 400 years ago. That's because of the distorting effects of our atmosphere. The Hubble Space Telescope (HST), carried into space by a shuttle in 1990, orbits above Earth's atmosphere and has allowed us to see clearer and farther than ever before. Thanks to Hubble, we've seen star nurseries and suspected planets outside our solar system and found out that the universe contains a lot more galaxies than we thought.

DOING THE ACTIVITY

1. Engage students in a discussion about telescopes. Ask: Why do you think big telescopes are put on top of mountains and out in deserts? *(The atmosphere is thinner on top of mountains and less humid in deserts.)* Tell students that the air surrounding the Earth distorts our view of space. It's like looking through water. Ask: Why can a space telescope see clearer and farther? *(It's high above the Earth's atmosphere.)*

2. Photocopy and distribute page 37 to each student. Have them browse the Web to view photographs taken by the Hubble Space Telescope.

3. Tell students that they will create postcards using a photo taken by the Hubble Space Telescope. If necessary, help them print their pictures. Provide students with scissors and paste to help them assemble their postcards.

More To Do:
Hubble History

Shuttle astronauts had to repair the Hubble in 1993 and 1999. They have also updated its instruments a number of times since it was launched. Have student pairs find out more about the early "trouble with Hubble" and how it was repaired.

Name(s) _____ **Date** _____

Postcard from Space

Choose and print a favorite picture snapped by the Hubble Space Telescope from the Web. Read about the picture by clicking on its caption. Cut out the postcard below and paste the picture on the other side of the card. Then fill out the postcard and "send" it to your classmates.

✂ -

Dear _____,

This is a picture of _____. It's

_____

away from Earth. The Hubble Space Telescope

took this picture in the year _____. The

image is really cool because

_____

_____

_____

_____

Love,

_____

TO:

_____

_____

_____

_____

Language
Arts
Careers

Wanted: Astronaut

Students read about astronauts and write classified ads for astronaut pilots and mission specialists.

BACKGROUND

NASA chooses about 20 astronaut candidates every two years. In general they look for knowledgeable and skilled people who learn fast, are in good health, can stay cool under stressful situations, and work well with others in cramped quarters. Most shuttle astronauts are either pilots or mission specialists. *Pilots* primarily fly the shuttle, while *mission specialists* conduct experiments, make space walks, and repair and launch satellites and other spacecraft.

DOING THE ACTIVITY

1. Photocopy and distribute page 39 to each student or student pair. (Note: If student pairs are doing the activity, considering having one read and write about pilots and the other about mission specialists.) As a class, discuss the different points on the chart. What education, experience, and personal qualities do students think astronauts need?

2. Have students read about astronauts on the Web and take notes. Then have them write help-wanted ads away from the computer. Post the ads on a bulletin board or wall.

More To Do:

Astronaut Biographies

Invite students to pick a favorite astronaut and write about his or her life.

Name(s) _____

Date _____

Jobs in Space

On the Web, find out what it takes to become an astronaut candidate. Fill out the chart about the two astronaut jobs below. Then write an ad for a NASA pilot and mission specialist on the back of this page.

	PILOT	MISSION SPECIALIST
Job responsibilities		
Education needed		
Experience needed		
Physical requirements		
Personal qualities		
Other requirements		

Science

Space Suit Search

Students learn about space suits and design one for the first crewed Mars mission.

BACKGROUND

There's no atmosphere in space, so astronauts take one with them—a space suit. Space suits are generally airtight and pressurized, and temperature- and humidity-controlled. They also protect against heat, radiation, and small flying debris, have a water supply and waste-disposal system, and are flexible enough to allow movement for work tasks. But space suits vary depending on the particular conditions they'll encounter. The Apollo moon-landing suits were made of 17 protective layers including Teflon-coated glass fiber, aluminum-coated plastic, and rubber. The shuttle astronauts, on the other hand, wear relatively flimsy reentry suits that primarily moderate pressure changes.

DOING THE ACTIVITY

1. Photocopy and distribute page 41 to each student. Invite students to choose the type of suit they wish to design or assign them one of the three types listed on the student page.

2. Encourage students to visit the Web to learn more about space suits and their designs. Then have them fill out the chart to plan their design.

3. Provide students with art materials to draw and label their designs away from the computer.

4. Invite students who designed space suits for the same purpose to compare designs. If time permits, challenge them to create a "second generation" design as a group that incorporates their shared ideas.

More To Do:

Suit Up!

Gather a few long balloons and blow them up.
Ask a volunteer to help you demonstrate what it feels like to wear a space suit. Put two balloons on each of the student's arms and hold them in place with large rubber bands or string. Put one balloon on the inside of the elbow, and the other on the outside. Have the student try to bend his or her arms. How does it feel? Ask: How difficult do you think it is for astronauts to move in thick space suits?

Dressing for Mars

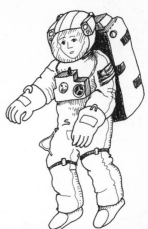

Find out about space suits from the Web: Why do astronauts need them? What does a space suit do? Are all space suits the same? Think about the first crewed mission to Mars. Design a space suit for a mission to Mars. Fill the chart below, then draw and label your spacesuit on the back of this sheet.

Name of space suit: _____

What will it be used for? (circle one)
★ Spacewalking for ship repair
★ Walking on Mars surface
★ Earth re-entry & Mars entry

What conditions are astronauts likely to face during their mission?	**What parts or features does a space suit need to adapt to these conditions?**

Science
Social
Studies

Space in Time

Students complete a time line of historic space events using Web sites.

BACKGROUND

Space flight and exploration history isn't an old story. The first rocket to make it into outer space was launched just over 50 years ago and no human has yet set foot on another planet. Many space firsts are well-remembered recent events of the 20th century, and much of space history still remains to be made. The history of space exploration is filled with tragedy, drama, and celebration, and has lots of great stories behind every milestone.

DOING THE ACTIVITY

1. Prepare students for the activity by asking them a few space trivia questions, such as: Which country sent the first artificial satellite in space? *(U.S.S.R.)* When was the first moon landing? *(1969)*

2. Photocopy and distribute page 43 to each student. Have students conduct research on the Web to complete their time lines.

3. Challenge students to add extra facts to their time lines or have groups create more comprehensive time lines on a bulletin board or wall.

ANSWERS

1957—Sputnik	1961—Yuri Gagarin	1969—Apollo 11
1977—Voyager	1981—Columbia	1986—Mir

1990—Hubble Space Telescope

1998—International Space Station

More To Do:

My Mission Patch

Mission patches are a great NASA tradition.
Challenge students to design a mission patch for a future crewed mission.
They can draw or paint the patch or use art software such as Kid Pix.

Space Time Line

When did humans first land on the moon? Who was the first person in space?
Conduct research on the Web to fill in the missing information in the time line below.

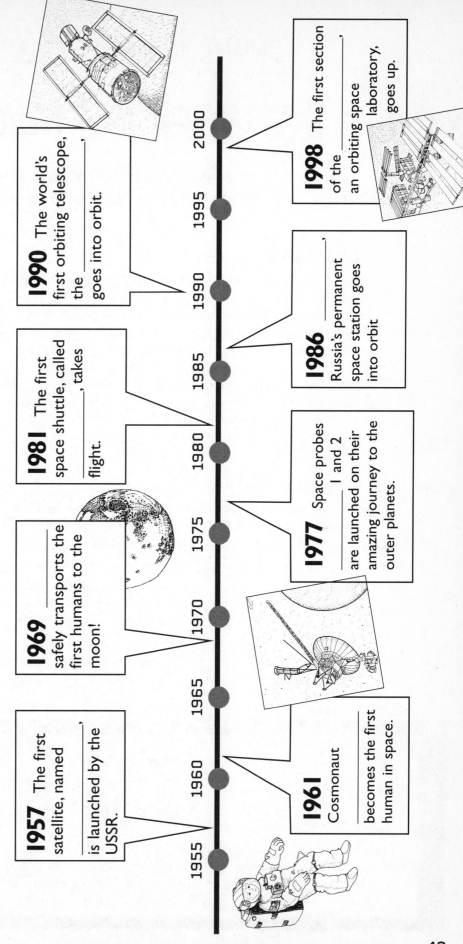

1957 The first satellite, named _____ is launched by the USSR.

1961 Cosmonaut _____ becomes the first human in space.

1969 _____ safely transports the first humans to the moon!

1977 Space probes 1 and 2 _____ are launched on their amazing journey to the outer planets.

1981 The first space shuttle, called _____, takes _____ flight.

1986 Russia's permanent space station _____ goes into orbit

1990 The world's first orbiting telescope, the _____, goes into orbit.

1998 The first section of the _____, an orbiting space laboratory, goes up.

1955 1960 1965 1970 1975 1980 1985 1990 1995 2000

Science
Critical
Thinking

Design an ISS Module

Students access the latest information on the International Space Station and design a module for it.

BACKGROUND

The International Space Station (ISS) is a work in progress. Scheduled for completion in 2004, it will be bigger than a soccer field, have nearly an acre of solar panels, and weigh more than a million pounds. This cooperative effort of 16 nations is the largest spacecraft ever built. The ISS orbits 244 miles (407 km) above Earth and is being assembled module by module, each one transported to the station by rocket or space shuttle. Once there, the modules are assembled using robotic arms and spacewalking astronauts. A total of 43 flights will be needed to complete the station. The modules hold solar arrays, living quarters, and science labs.

DOING THE ACTIVITY

1. As a class, discuss the International Space Station. Assess students' knowledge of the station, including its purpose—to serve as an international science laboratory in space.

2. Photocopy and distribute page 45 to each student group.

3. Encourage students to explore the Web to study the different modules that make up the ISS. Then have them brainstorm other modules that might be useful for the space station.

4. Invite students to fill out their charts and draw their modules away from the computer. You'll need to provide them with art materials for drawing.

More To Do:

Get a Grip

Invite students to try working like spacewalking astronauts assembling the ISS. Have them put on two sets of bulky gloves. Then challenge them to do tasks that test their dexterity, such as picking up toothpicks, coins, or other small items; turning a screw or bolt with a tool; or signing their name.

Name(s) _____ Date _____

My Space Station Module

The International Space Station (ISS) is made up of many sections, called modules. What module would you add? Check out the different ISS modules and their purpose on the Web. Then think about what module you would add to the space station. Write your plans below, then draw the module on the back of this sheet.

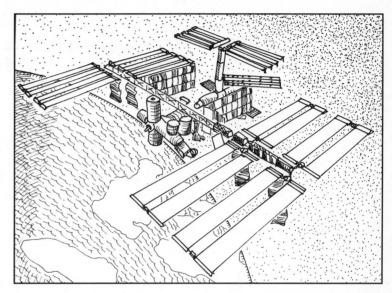

Name of module: _____

What does it do? _____

_____

Why is it needed? _____

_____

_____

What would it look like? _____

_____

_____

Tour the Air and Space Museum

Social Studies Language Arts

Students take a virtual tour of the National Air and Space Museum, then write a tour-guide script of one of its galleries.

BACKGROUND

The Smithsonian Institution's National Air and Space Museum (NASM) has the largest collection of aircraft and spacecraft in the world. Among the artifacts are the original Wright brothers' 1903 *Flyer*, the *Spirit of St. Louis*, *Apollo 11* command module, and a lunar rock sample that museum visitors can touch. The museum, which is located on the National Mall in Washington, D.C., is also an important research center.

DOING THE ACTIVITY

1. Ask students: If you were to build a space museum, what would you put in it? List students' responses on the board.

2. Photocopy and distribute page 47 to each student, student pair, or small group doing the activity.

3. Let students click through the map on the NASM Web site to get a feel for the museum. (Note: You can skip this step if time is limited.) Then have students choose a gallery online, or assign a gallery to each student or student group.

4. Ask students to fill in their charts at the computer. They can write their scripts away from the computer on the back of their sheets.

More To Do:

Rocket Science

Challenge students to research what made spaceflight possible—rockets. They can collect pictures of rockets and create a time line that shows the evolution of rockets through history.

Name(s) _____ Date _____

Welcome to the Air and Space Museum

Visit the Space Galleries Web site and choose a gallery to write about. Click on the gallery and look at the exhibits and artifacts featured there. Use the chart below to take some notes on your favorite exhibits. Then write a tour-guide script using the information you've gathered.

Tour Guide Script for Gallery _____

Exhibit/Artifact #1:

_____

What's interesting about it?

_____

_____

Exhibit/Artifact #2:

_____

What's interesting about it?

_____

_____

Exhibit/Artifact #3:

_____

What's interesting about it?

_____

_____

Exhibit/Artifact #4:

_____

What's interesting about it?

_____

_____

Resources

Books, Software, Videos, and Web sites about space.

Teacher Resources

Compton's Learning Astronomy (The Learning Company). Visit distant galaxies, ride spectacular comets, and explore mysterious realms with this desk-top planetarium that features interactive tutorials and customizable controls.

How the Universe Works by Heather Couper (Reader's Digest, 1994). This book's clearly laid-out activities range in difficulty from taking a core sample of an ice-cream bar with a drinking straw to build-ing a model of the Galileo space probe.

Cosmic Science by Jim Wiese (John Wiley, 1997). The "Over 40 Gravity-Defying, Earth-Orbiting, Space-Cruising Activities for Kids" use low-tech materials to teach high-tech science.

Space Encyclopedia by Heather Couper (Dorling Kindersley, 1999). This gorgeous Eyewitness book covers cosmology, astrophysics, astronomy, and space exploration with thousands of photos, graphics, maps, and charts.

Space.com www.space.com

NASA Homepage www.nasa.gov

NASA Quest quest.arc.nasa.gov

NASAKIDS Teacher's Corner kids.msfc.nasa.gov/Teachers

Science Education Gateway cse.ssl.berkeley.edu/segway

Student Resources

Magic School Bus Explores the Solar System (Microsoft). Join Ms. Frizzle and her class as they take a field trip into the solar system, visit the planets, and conduct cool science experiments.

National Geographic's Asteroids: Deadly Impact (National Geographic, 1997). Join extraordinary scientists Eugene and Carolyn Shoemaker as they remap the heavens with their discoveries of more than 30 comets and hundreds of asteroids.

Nova: To the Moon (WGBH Video, 1999). This two-hour PBS Nova special tells the story of the Apollo program and its triumphant moon landing through interviews of Apollo Project members.

Find the Constellations by Hans Augusto Rey (Houghton Mifflin, 1980). A nicely illustrated, informative beginner's guide to locating and identifying constella-tions in the northern hemisphere. Includes a glossary and timetable for sky viewing.

Astronomy Smart Junior: The Science of the Solar System and Beyond by Michael L. Bentley (Princeton Review, 1996). Fun activities and clear information are presented as Bridget, Babette, Barnaby, and Beauregard take kids on a tour of the solar system, including stops at colonies on the moon and Mars.

StarChild starchild.gsfc.nasa.gov/docs /StarChild/StarChild.html

NASAKIDS kids.msfc.nasa.gov

Spacekids.com spacekids.com